KOYOHARU GOTOUGE

They're publishing a graphic novel by me! Thank you! And heartfelt thanks to all the readers, my editors over the years, my assistants, everyone in the *Jump* editorial department, everyone at the printer, the people who designed the book, and the many other people who have offered their help!

DEMON SLAYER: KIMETSU NO YAIBA VOLUME 1
Shonen Jump Edition

Story and Art by
KOYOHARU GOTOUGE

KIMETSU NO YAIBA
© 2016 by Koyoharu Gotouge
All rights reserved. First published in Japan
in 2016 by SHUEISHA Inc., Tokyo. English
translation rights arranged by SHUEISHA Inc.

TRANSLATION John Werry

ENGLISH ADAPTATION Stan!

TOUCH-UP ART & LETTERING John Hunt

DESIGN Adam Grano

EDITOR Mike Montesa

Printed in Italy

Published by VIZ Media, LLC
P.O. Box 77010
San Francisco, CA 94107

33
First printing, July 2018
Thirty-third printing, July 2024

viz.com

1

CRUELTY

DEMON SLAYER

KIMETSU NO YAIBA

KOYOHARU GOTOUGE

CONTENTS

CRUELTY

HOW DID THIS HAPPEN?

CHAPTER 1: CRUELTY

YOUR BIG BROTHER IS DEFINITELY GOING TO SAVE YOU!

NEZUKO...

DON'T DIE.

DON'T DIE.

YOU CAN'T DIE.

I'M GONNA SAVE YOU.

CHAPTER 1: CRUELTY

TANJIRO!

IT'S SNOWING AND IT'S DANGEROUS.

YOU DON'T HAVE TO GO.

YOUR FACE IS PITCH-BLACK.

COME HERE.

THANK YOU.

...EVEN IF IT'S JUST A LITTLE.

I WANT US TO HAVE A GREAT NEW YEAR'S FEAST, SO I'LL GO SELL AS MUCH CHARCOAL AS I CAN...

WHAAAA?!

I WANNA GO TOO!

TANJIRO, ARE YOU GOING TO TOWN AGAIN TODAY?

...SO HE CAN'T PULL YOU WHEN YOU'RE TIRED.

HE ISN'T TAKING THE CART TODAY...

BUT MOM!

NO.

NO. YOU CAN'T WALK FAST LIKE TANJIRO.

...I WAS HOPING WE'D DO IT TOGETHER.

I WILL, BUT...

I wanna go with you!

TAKEO...

I KNOW YOU CAN'T DO A LOT, BUT CUT A LITTLE WOOD TODAY. OKAY?

BE CARE-FUL!

HURRY BACK, OKAY?

I WAS PUTTING ROKUTA TO SLEEP...

NEZUKO...

...BUT I HEARD ALL THE COMMO-TION.

TANJIRO!

SEE YOU LATER!

...SO THEY'VE STARTED CLINGING TO YOU.

THEY'VE BEEN SO LONELY SINCE FATHER DIED...

IT'S ALWAYS CHANGING.

BUT LIFE IS LIKE THE WEATHER...

OUR LIFE ISN'T EASY, BUT WE'RE HAPPY.

...AND THE SNOW WON'T ALWAYS KEEP FALLING.

IT WON'T ALWAYS BE EASY...

...THE SMELL OF BLOOD IN THE AIR.

WHEN HAPPINESS ENDS THERE'S ALWAYS...

OH, TANJIRO!

THANKS FOR FIXING MY SHOJI DOOR THE OTHER DAY!

YOU'LL CATCH A COLD!

YOU CAME DOWN THE MOUNTAIN ON A DAY LIKE TODAY? YOU WORK SO HARD!

GIVE ME SOME CHARCOAL TOO!

HEY! SELL ME SOME CHARCOAL!

HELP ME!

SHE SAYS I BROKE A DISH!

SMELL IT!

YOU'RE JUST IN TIME!

AAAH! TANJIRO!

WILL YOU HELP ME CARRY SOME BUNDLES?!

TANJIRO!

I TOLD YOU IT WASN'T ME!

A CAT? OH DEAR.

I SMELL A CAT.

SEEEE?!

WHEW! IT'S GETTING LATE!

TP TP TP TP

IT'S TOO DANGEROUS!

HEY, TAN-JIRO! YOU AREN'T...

...GOING BACK UP THE MOUNTAIN ARE YOU?!

14

BUT...

IT'S ALL RIGHT. YOU'RE WELCOME HERE.

YOU CAN STAY HERE.

COME BACK.

PLEASE.

I'VE GOT A GOOD NOSE FOR TROUBLE. I'LL BE FINE.

YOU DON'T WANT TO RUN INTO ANY *DEMONS*.

EAT, THEN SLEEP. YOU CAN GET UP AND GO HOME EARLY TOMORROW.

SO YOU SHOULDN'T WALK AROUND AT NIGHT.

FOR AGES...

... MAN-EATING DEMONS HAVE ROAMED THESE WOODS AFTER DARK.

YES...

...THEY CAN.

CAN'T THE DEMONS COME INSIDE HOUSES?

BUT...

BECAUSE *DEMON SLAYERS* CUT THEM DOWN.

HAVE FOR AGES...

...WHY DON'T THEY EAT EVERY-ONE?

...THEN...

BUT...

THERE'S NO NEED TO FEAR. THERE'S NO SUCH THING AS DEMONS.

NEXT TIME, I'LL BRING MY LITTLE BROTHERS.

OLD MAN SABURO LIVES ALONE BECAUSE HE LOST HIS FAMILY. HE MUST BE LONELY.

BUT NOW THAT I THINK OF IT...

...MY GRANDMOTHER SAID THE SAME THING BEFORE SHE DIED.

...THE SMELL OF BLOOD IN THE AIR.

WHEN HAPPI-NESS ENDS THERE'S ALWAYS...

HFF

HFF

WHAT HAP—

WHAT HAPPENED?!

AGH!

WHAT THE...?

ROKUTA
...

NEZUKO
...

TAKEO...

SHIGERU
...

MOTHER
...

HANAKO
...

MAYBE A DOCTOR CAN SAVE HER.

ONLY NEZUKO'S BODY WAS STILL WARM.

MAYBE A BEAR TOO HUNGRY TO HIBERNATE?

HOW DID THIS HAPPEN? A BEAR?

KEEP GOING!

MOVE YOUR FEET FASTER.

THE AIR'S SO COLD IT'S FREEZING MY LUNGS.

SO HARD TO BREATHE!

I HAVE TO SAVE YOU.

I WON'T LET YOU DIE.

TWITCH

IT'S STILL A LONG WAY TO TOWN.

YOUR BIG BROTHER WILL SAVE YOU!

AAAAH!

GRRAAA

SHWF

?!

WHMP

I'M SLIP—

OH NO!

THE SNOW...

...SAVED ME.

BUT IT ALSO MADE ME SLIP!

NEZUKO!

!!

YOU SHOULDN'T BE UP!

...CARRY YOU INTO TOWN!

LET ME...

NEZUKO!

ARE YOU ALL RIGHT?

SHF

NEZUKO ...

WH WMPH

OMP

CH

I THOUGHT OF WHAT OLD MAN SABURO SAID.

WAS NEZUKO...

...A MAN-EATING DEMON?

A DEMON!

NEZUKO HAS BEEN HUMAN...

...SINCE THE DAY SHE WAS BORN.

NO, THAT WAS IM-POSSIBLE.

...FALLEN OVER ROKUTA, LIKE SHE WAS PROTECTING HIM.

BUT NEZUKO COULDN'T HAVE DONE ALL THAT. I FOUND HER...

BUT THIS NEZUKO...

...SMELLS OF BLOOD AND DEATH.

WHOOMP

SHE DIDN'T HAVE ANY BLOOD ON HER MOUTH OR HANDS.

AND THERE'S YET...

SKRRZ

SHFF

SKRK

...ANOTHER SMELL...

26

...AND SHE'S GETTING STRONGER!

...SHE'S GROWING BIGGER...

WHAT-EVER THE REASON...

...HAPPENED TO MY WHOLE FAMILY.

WHILE I WAS SAFELY ASLEEP IN TOWN, SOMETHING HORRIBLE...

BUT SHE'S SO STRONG! I CAN'T PUSH HER AWAY!

NEZUKO!

I HAVE TO SAVE NEZUKO IF I CAN!

HOW THEY MUST HAVE SUFFERED.

...AND I WASN'T THERE TO HELP THEM.

BE STRONG!

YOU CAN DO IT!

DON'T TURN INTO A DEMON!

FIGHT IT! FIGHT FOR YOUR LIFE!

HOLD ON, NEZUKO!

PLIP

PLIP

PLIP

NEZUKO!

SNAP

FWSH

WHO...

FMP

WHO IS THAT?

*AKKIMESSATSU,
DESTROYER OF DEMONS

A KATANA...

WHY
DO YOU
PROTECT
HER?

GRAAAR

S-SISTER...

SHE'S MY...

...LITTLE SISTER!

THAT IS YOUR LITTLE SISTER?

RAAGH

GRAAH

SNATCH

DASH

...

HW SH !

DON'T MOVE.

WAIT! NEZUKO HASN'T KILLED ANYONE!

SO OF COURSE, I'LL TAKE YOUR LITTLE SISTER'S HEAD TOO.

KILLING DEMONS IS MY JOB.

THAT MUST BE WHO KILLED EVERYONE!

...FROM SOMEONE I'VE NEVER SMELLED BEFORE!

THERE WAS A SCENT AT MY HOUSE...

THAT'S EASY. DEMON BLOOD GOT IN HER WOUND, SO SHE'S TRANSFORMED INTO A DEMON.

GRAAR!

NOT NEZUKO!

BUT...

I DON'T KNOW WHAT'S MAKING HER ACT LIKE THIS...

THAT IS HOW MAN-EATING DEMONS MULTIPLY.

NO! I'M SURE SHE KNOWS WHO I AM!

A MOMENT AGO SHE ALMOST ATE *YOU!*

NEZUKO WOULD NEVER EAT ANYONE!

I'LL MAKE HER *HUMAN* AGAIN!

I'LL FIND A WAY TO *CURE* HER!

I *WON'T* LET HER HURT ANYONE!

I'LL FIND A WAY! I *SWEAR!* PLEASE DON'T KILL HER!

A HUMAN WHO BECOMES A DEMON CANNOT GO BACK.

SHE WON'T GET BETTER.

SH N N NG

...SO...

...SO...

I'LL ALSO FIND THE ONE THAT KILLED MY FAMILY!

I'LL DO ALL THAT, SO...

36

I CAN'T LOSE NEZUKO TOO!

STOP!

PLEASE, STOP.

PLEASE...

PLEASE DON'T KILL MY LITTLE SISTER!

PLEASE...

NEVER LEAVE YOURSELF SO *DEFENSELESS* IN FRONT OF AN ENEMY!

STOP BOWING SO PITIFULLY!

IF THAT WORKED, YOUR FAMILY WOULD STILL BE ALIVE!

FL IN CH

...CURE HIS LITTLE SISTER?

OR EVEN *FIND* HIS ENEMY?

HOW CAN A WEAKLING LIKE YOU, WHO BOWS DOWN WHEN IT'S TIME TO FIGHT, TO KILL OR BE KILLED... HOW CAN SUCH A MAN...

...*YOU MUST FIGHT FOR IT!*

IF YOU WANT SOME-THING...

DEMONS MIGHT KNOW HOW TO CURE YOUR LITTLE SISTER...

...NO DEMON WILL RESPECT YOUR WHINING AND BEGGING!

... BUT ...

THE MEEK HAVE NO POWER AND NO OPTIONS!

THE STRONG WILL CRUSH THEM IN EVERY WAY!

BEFORE...

WHY DID YOU COVER YOUR SISTER?

DID YOU THINK THAT WOULD PROTECT HER?!

AND FOR THAT MATTER, I DON'T RESPECT YOU EITHER!

THAT'S REALITY!

THAT'S HOW I WAS ABLE TO TAKE HER!

WHY DIDN'T YOU THROW YOUR HATCHET?

WHY DID YOU SHOW ME YOUR BACK?!

HFF

HFF

HFF

GRAAH!

I SHOULD HAVE SKEWERED YOU BOTH!

THUD

YOUR HEART IS CRUSHED.

YOUR FAMILY IS DEAD AND YOUR SISTER HAS BECOME A DEMON.

I KNOW YOUR PAIN, HOW YOU MUST WANT TO CRY OUT.

DON'T CRY.

DON'T DESPAIR.

THOSE THINGS WILL DO YOU NO GOOD.

BUT THERE IS NO TURNING BACK TIME.

...YOUR FAMILY MIGHT HAVE SURVIVED.

IF I'D COME HALF A DAY SOONER...

ANGER THAT BECOMES THE UNWAVERING FORCE THAT DRIVES YOUR LIMBS.

...THAT GIVES NO QUARTER.

STRONG, PURE ANGER...

FILL YOUR HEART WITH ANGER.

...CANNOT PROTECT YOUR SISTER OR FIND HER A CURE.

AND THEY CERTAINLY CANNOT AVENGE YOUR FAMILY.

WEAKNESS AND EMPTY PROMISES ...

W...

SH NK

AAAAH!

WHOK

WHAT A FOOL!

A SIMPLE, HEAD-ON ATTACK RELYING ON PURE EMOTION.

THOK

JUST BEFORE PASSING BEHIND THE TREE, HE THREW A ROCK...

...AND WHILE HIDDEN BY THE TREE HE THREW HIS HATCHET.

...WAS TO STRIKE ME DOWN AFTER I KILLED HIM.

HE KNEW HE COULDN'T WIN AGAINST ME, SO HIS PLAN...

HE HID HIS HAND SO I WOULDN'T SEE HE WAS UNARMED.

GRAAR!

THIS KID...

WHOK

NO! I'M TOO LATE!

SHE'S ABOUT TO EAT HIM!

NEZUKO...

NEZUKO WOULD NEVER EAT ANYONE!

NOT NEZUKO!

HE WOULDN'T BE...

...THE FIRST TO SAY THAT AND THEN GET EATEN ANYWAY.

BECAUSE THEY NEED THE ENERGY.

I'VE SEEN IT COUNTLESS TIMES.

STARVING DEMONS WILL KILL AND EAT THEIR OWN PARENTS AND SIBLINGS.

...AND MUST WANT TO EAT HUMAN FLESH AS SOON AS POSSIBLE.

...NOT TO MENTION THE STRENGTH IT TOOK TO TRANSFORM INTO A DEMON. SHE MUST BE DOUBLY STARVED RIGHT NOW...

THIS GIRL IS INJURED. IT COSTS HER STRENGTH...

...TO HEAL THAT WOUND...

...AND FOCUSING HER ANGER ON ME.

BUT SHE'S PROTECTING HIM...

YOU'RE AWAKE?

TELL HIM THAT *GIYU TOMIOKA* SENT YOU.

GO SEE AN OLD MAN NAMED *SAKONJI UROKODAKI* WHO LIVES AT THE FOOT OF MOUNT SAGIRI.

...BUT DON'T LET HER INTO DIRECT SUNLIGHT.

YOUR SISTER SHOULD BE FINE BECAUSE THE SUN ISN'T OUT TODAY...

CHAPTER 2: THE STRANGER

...AND A LITTLE STRAW AND BAMBOO?

I BEG YOUR PARDON...

...BUT MAY I TAKE THAT BASKET...

THAT'S ALL RIGHT. CAN I PAY YOU?

NO NEED. IT'S A BROKEN BASKET.

...BUT THE BASKET HAS A HOLE IN IT.

WE DON'T MIND...

WE DON'T WANT IT!

BUT I *WANT* TO PAY!

WHAT A STUBBORN KID!

NO, THANK YOU.

SHAKE SHAKE

PLEASE LET ME PAY.

YOU CAN HAVE THE OTHER STUFF TOO.

JUST TAKE IT! IT'S ONLY A FEW COINS ANYWAY!

OWWW!

THANK YOU VERY MUCH!

SHE'S GONE!

HMM?

NEZUKO!

NEZUKO...

...

POP

THERE SHE IS!

JUST WAIT.

SHE MUST REALLY NOT WANT THE SUNLIGHT TO HIT HER. HER FACE IS SCRUNCHED UP.

MY SISTER IS LIKE A MOLE NOW.

DID SHE DIG THAT HOLE?

TA-DAH!

FWIK

FWIK

FWIK

...

GET IN.

HERE.

THE BASKET.

I WANT US TO TRAVEL DURING THE DAY.

I'LL CARRY YOU.

WILL YOU FIT IN HERE?

NEZUKO HAS GROWN UP.

I STILL THINK SHE'S A LITTLE GIRL.

YOU'RE TOO BIG.

...RE-VERSE THAT...

...AND GET SMALLER?

...YOU'RE AS BIG AS AN ADULT. CAN YOU...

NEZUKO ...

HMM?

STUFF

AH!

GET SMALLER!

NEZUKO.

SMALLER.

FLOP

FLOP

EWUP

YEOW!

OH! GOOD!

KAW

KAW

GOOD GIRL, NEZUKO!

I'M IMPRESSED!

PAT PAT

THAT'S PERFECT!

THE SUN WILL SET SOON.

AND YOU'RE GOING TO CARRY THAT HUGE LOAD? IT'S DANGEROUS.

TO GET TO MOUNT SAGIRI, YOU FIRST HAVE TO CROSS THAT MOUNTAIN.

...SO DON'T GET LOST!

PEOPLE REALLY DO DISAPPEAR UP THERE...

THANK YOU VERY MUCH.

BOW

I'LL BE PLENTY CAREFUL.

OH!

!!

I SMELL BLOOD!

THERE'S A WAY STATION.

THERE'S A LIGHT ON. SOMEONE MUST BE THERE.

LET'S GO.

ARE YOU ALL RIGHT?

THESE MOUNTAIN PATHS ARE DANGEROUS. THAT TRAVELER MAY BE INJURED!

KLAK

KT K

GET AWAY FROM MY FEEDING GROUND!

...IS MY TERRITORY!

THIS...

WHAT?!

HEY!

...

HMM...?

SOMETHING'S WRONG HERE.

PLP PLP PLP

A MAN-EATING DEMON!

ARE YOU TWO HUMAN?

HA! HA!

A HATCHET?!

HA!

NOT BAD!

FWMP

SEE?

THE BLEEDING ALREADY STOPPED!

BUT A WOUND LIKE THIS...

...WILL HEAL IN NO TIME!

VWP

ZWP. ZWP

?!

SH-SHE JUST KILLED HIM! WELL, HE WAS A DEMON, SO...

WHY YOUUU ...!

I CAN'T BELIEVE IT! IT JUST MOVED WITH ITS HEAD RIPPED OFF!

WHAT ARE A DEMON AND A HUMAN DOING TOGETHER?!

I KNEW IT! ONE OF YOU IS A DEMON!

SOMETHING DIDN'T SEEM RIGHT!

Tmp Tmp Tmp

IT'S STILL TALK-ING!!

MY HAIR IS TANGLED UP ON THE HAFT! AND I GREW THESE HANDS TOO SHORT, SO I CAN'T GET A GRIP!

ARGH!

HE PINNED ME TO THE TREE WITH HIS HATCHET!!

NEZUKO!

WHSH

GYAAAH!

SPLAT

WOW!

HOW MANY DEMONS ARE THERE?

SHNG

SO I HAVE TO DO THIS.

HFF

HFF

BUT...

...IF I DON'T KILL HIM, HE'LL ATTACK MORE PEOPLE.

HFF

HFF

A DIFFERENT DEMON.

HE SMELLS DIFFERENT THAN THE ONE THAT WAS AT MY HOUSE.

DO IT!

...LORD SAKONJI UROKODAKI.

GREETINGS ...

A DEMON SLAUGHTERED HIS FAMILY...

HE HAD THE COURAGE TO FIGHT ME UNARMED.

I HAVE SENT A BOY YOUR WAY WHO SAYS HE WANTS TO BECOME A DEMON-SLAYING SWORDSMAN.

...BUT SHE CHOOSES NOT TO ATTACK HUMANS.

...TRANSFORMING HIS SURVIVING SISTER INTO A DEMON...

I BELIEVE THAT PERHAPS...

LIKE YOU, THE BOY HAS A STRONG SENSE OF SMELL.

I SENSE SOMETHING IN THESE TWO THAT IS DIFFERENT FROM THE OTHERS.

I KNOW THIS IS A SELFISH REQUEST, SO PLEASE FORGIVE ME.

...HE COULD BE WORTHY OF CARRYING ON YOUR TRADITIONS.

PLEASE, TRAIN HIM.

SIN-CERELY...

...GIYU TOMIOKA.

...AND IN GOOD SPIRITS.

MAY THIS FIND YOU IN GOOD HEALTH...

DON'T TRUST WHAT OTHERS SAY.

CAN'T YOU SOLVE THIS RIDDLE YOURSELF?

HE MOVED IN COMPLETE SILENCE.

H...

HOW *CAN* I FINISH *IT* OFF?

A TENGU MASK!

I'LL HAVE TO CRUSH THE HEAD...

...

NNGH

IF STAB-BING IT WON'T WORK...

ISN'T THERE ANY WAY TO KILL IT WITH ONE BLOW?

TO COMPLETELY CRUSH THE HEAD, I'LL HAVE TO SMASH IT WITH A ROCK REPEATEDLY.

IT WILL SURELY SUFFER.

SNIFF

WHEN FACING A DEMON, HE STILL REEKS OF SYMPATHY AND CONSIDERATION.

HE EVEN FEELS SYMPATHY FOR A DEMON.

HIS KINDNESS PREVENTS HIM FROM TAKING DECISIVE ACTION.

DAMN...

...THIS KID IS NO GOOD.

I WAS UNCONSCIOUS.

I FEEL SICK.

IS MY BODY DEAD?

...THIS BOY IS USELESS.

GIYU...

WHA—?

...

JUST A TOUCH OF SUNLIGHT DID THAT?!

NO WONDER NEZUKO FEARS IT!

OH, YEAH...

...THAT GUY.

UM...

HE'S BURYING THE DEMON'S VICTIMS.

YOU
THINK
TOO
SLOWLY!

!!

WHY COULDN'T YOU ANSWER THAT QUESTION IMMEDIATELY?

...

YOU COULD NEVER FINISH OFF A DEMON BEFORE THE MORNING LIGHT.

YOU STRUGGLE OVER THE SIMPLEST DECISIONS.

YOU ARE TOO SOFT!

THAT IS WHAT IT MEANS TO TRAVEL WITH YOUR SISTER WHO HAS BECOME A DEMON!

WHEN YOUR SISTER EATS SOMEONE, THERE ARE *TWO THINGS* YOU HAVE TO DO...

KILL YOUR SISTER... THEN SLIT YOUR OWN *BELLY* AND DIE!

DO YOU UNDER-STAND WHAT I AM SAYING?

YOUR SISTER MUST *NEVER* TAKE THE LIFE...

...OF AN INNOCENT PERSON!

BUT IT IS YOUR SACRED DUTY TO ENSURE THAT THIS *NEVER* HAPPENS.

VERY WELL...

...I WILL TEST YOU TO SEE IF YOU HAVE WHAT IT TAKES...

...TO BE A DEMON-SLAYER SWORDSMAN.

YES!

SHOULDER YOUR SISTER AND FOLLOW ME.

AND HIS FEET REALLY DON'T MAKE ANY SOUND!

HFF

HFF

HF

HE'S FAST!

HOW OLD IS THIS GUY?!

...SUFFERING IS ALL YOU'VE EVER KNOWN...

...LITTLE SISTER.

BUT THEN...

...THIS'LL BE ROUGH, BUT HANG IN THERE!

NEZUKO...

...TO GIVE THE YOUNGER KIDS PLENTY TO EAT.

INSTEAD, I USE THAT MONEY...

ARE YOU MENDING YOUR KIMONO AGAIN?

YOU SHOULD BUY A NEW ONE.

NO, NO...

I LIKE THIS KIMONO!

...I'M FINE.

EVERYTHING I COULDN'T GIVE TO THEM, I'LL GIVE TO YOU!

I WILL MAKE YOU HUMAN AGAIN!

AND THEN I'LL BUY YOU A BEAUTIFUL KIMONO!

THE TEST *BEGINS* NOW.

CLIMB THE MOUNTAIN.

...DID I...

...PASS THE TEST?

WHEEZ

WHEEZ

HFF

HFF

HFF

S...

SO...

FWIP

HFF

HFF

—I'M DIZZY...

I'M ALREADY TIRED. MY LEGS ARE GETTING WEAK.

HFF

HFF

THIS TIME, I WILL NOT WAIT UNTIL SUNRISE.

NOW YOU MUST DESCEND TO THE HOUSE AT THE FOOT OF THE MOUNTAIN.

HFF

HFF

OH, I GET IT.

HE THINKS I'LL GET LOST IN THIS THICK FOG.

IS THAT ALL?

HFF

HFF

GASP

HUH?

THAT'S EASY! I HAVE A SHARP NOSE!

I'VE ALREADY MEMORIZED UROKODAKI'S SCENT.

I JUST HAVE TO GET BACK BEFORE SUNRISE.

HFF

HFF

HFF

I GET IT!

A COVERED PIT!

THESE ARE ALL TRAPS.

THAT'S THE CHALLENGE!

WSH

UH-OH! HERE WE GO AGAIN!

MMPH

I'M IN BIG TROUBLE.

HFF

HFF

AND I JUST NOTICED... UP ON THIS MOUNTAIN...

IF I KEEP SETTING OFF EVERY TRAP, I WON'T GET DOWN THE MOUNTAIN BY MORNING.

HFF HFF HFF HFF

IT'S MUCH WORSE THAN THE MOUNTAIN WE LIVED ON!

...THE AIR'S SO THIN I CAN BARELY BREATHE!

CONTROL YOUR BREATHING. SNIFF OUT THE TRAPS.

I FEEL LIKE I MIGHT PASS OUT!

NO! I'VE GOTTA GET BACK!

THAT'S WHY I FEEL SO TIRED AND DIZZY.

YES! I CAN SMELL THEM!

TRAPS HAVE TO BE SET BY SOMEONE, AND THOSE SCENTS MUST LINGER.

...THE ABILITY TO EVADE THEM ALL!

BUT KNOWING THEY'RE THERE DOESN'T GRANT ME...

ZZZ

ZZZ

ZZZ

THUNK THUNK
THUNK

SHMP

SHMP

I...

...MADE IT...

...BACK.

HFF

HFF

HFF

...I ACCEPT YOU AS MY STUDENT!

TANJIRO KAMADO...

Taisho Whispers
& Rumors

○ 鬼滅奇譚 (*Mysterious Story of the Demon Slayer*)
(Kimetsu Kitan)

○ 鬼鬼滅滅 (*Demon Demon Slayer Slayer*)
(Kikimetsumetsu)

○ 悪鬼滅々 (*Evil Demon Slayer*)
(Akkimetsumetsu)

○ 鬼殺の刃 (*Sword of the Demon Killer*)
(Kisatsu no Yaiba)

○ 滅々鬼譚 (*Strange Tale of the Demon Slayer*)
(Metsumetsu Kitan)

○ 鬼殺譚 (*Tale of the Demon Killer*)
(Kisatsutan)

○ 空想鬼滅奇譚 (*The Fantastic Strange Tale of the Demon Slayer*)
(Kuso Kimetsu Kitan)

○ 鬼狩リカグツチ (*Demon Hunting God of Fire*)
(Onigari Kagutsuchi)

○ 炭のカグツチ (*Charred God of Fire*)
(Sumi no Kagutsuchi)

* "Kitan" means an unusual and mysterious story.

* "Kagutsuchi" is a god of fire.

Hello, I'm Gotoge.

I hear these titles were under consideration.

Which one do you like?

THERE ARE A FEW HUNDRED MEMBERS...

...OF THE DEMON SLAYER CORPS.

HOWEVER, THE IDENTITY OF THE LEADER OF THE DEMON SLAYER CORPS...

THE ORGANIZATION ISN'T OFFICIALLY RECOGNIZED BY THE GOVERNMENT.

...IS SHROUDED IN MYSTERY.

BUT IT HAS EXISTED SINCE DAYS OF OLD AND STILL HUNTS DEMONS TODAY.

THEY HAVE IMPRESSIVE PHYSICAL ABILITIES AND THEIR WOUNDS HEAL QUICKLY.

DEMONS.

STAPLE FOOD: HUMANS.

THEY CAN RECONNECT SEVERED FLESH AND GROW NEW LIMBS. SOME DEMONS CAN CHANGE FORM. OTHERS POSSESS STRANGE POWERS.

THEY KILL HUMANS AND EAT THEM.

IT IS UNCLEAR WHEN OR WHERE THEY FIRST APPEARED.

THE ONLY WAYS TO KILL THEM ARE BY EXPOSING THEM TO SUNLIGHT OR BY CUTTING OFF THEIR HEADS WITH A SPECIAL SWORD.

THEY ARE HUMAN, SO THEIR WOUNDS HEAL SLOWLY AND LOST LIMBS DO NOT RETURN.

THE DEMON SLAYER CORPS FIGHTS DEMONS FACE-TO-FACE.

NONETHELESS, THEY FIGHT DEMONS IN ORDER TO PROTECT ORDINARY PEOPLE.

THERE ARE MANY TRAINERS. IN DIFFERENT PLACES, THEY USE VARIOUS TRAINING METHODS.

I AM A TRAINER.

JUST LIKE IT SOUNDS, I TRAIN SWORDSMEN.

I DECIDE WHETHER YOU MAY ATTEMPT FINAL SELECTION.

IN ORDER TO JOIN THE DEMON SLAYER CORPS, YOU MUST SURVIVE THE FINAL SELECTION AT MOUNT FUJIKASANE.

AGAIN TODAY, I DESCENDED THE MOUNTAIN.

STARTING TODAY, I HAVE DECIDED TO WRITE THIS JOURNAL FOR NEZUKO.

I TRAIN AS HARD AS I CAN SO I WON'T DIE DURING FINAL SELECTION.

I'M GROWING STRONGER...

I GO DOWN THE MOUNTAIN REPEATEDLY, DAY AFTER DAY. I'VE BECOME QUITE GOOD AT AVOIDING TRAPS.

...AND MY NOSE IS EVEN SHARPER AT PICKING UP SCENTS.

IT'S LIKE HE REALLY WANTS TO KILL ME.

BUT THE TRAPS ARE GETTING MUCH DEADLIER.

IT REALLY GETS IN THE WAY...

...SO CARRYING IT GOT ME CAUGHT IN A LOT OF TRAPS.

TODAY, I WENT DOWN THE MOUNTAIN WITH A KATANA.

AFTER DESCENDING THE MOUNTAIN, I SWING THE SWORD SO MUCH I FEEL LIKE MY ARMS MIGHT FALL OFF.

SWSH

...715...

...716...

I SAY "TODAY," BUT LATELY I DO THIS EVERY DAY.

SWSH

TODAY, I PRACTICED SWINGING THE SWORD.

...713...

...714...

WITH A KATANA...

IT'S STRONG AGAINST FORCE LENGTHWISE BUT WEAK AGAINST FORCE FROM THE SIDE.

THE FIRST THING HE TAUGHT ME WAS THAT A KATANA BREAKS EASILY.

WHEN YOU SWING A KATANA...

...YOU MUST ATTACK STRAIGHT AHEAD.

...THE DIRECTION OF THE BLADE AND THE DIRECTION OF THE FORCE YOU APPLY MUST BE EXACTLY THE SAME.

...HE'LL BREAK MY BONES. HIS THREATS ARE COLD...

...LIKE THE MOUNTAIN.

IN OTHER WORDS, IF I BREAK IT...

...YOU!

FURTHER-MORE...

...IF YOU DAMAGE THE SWORD, HE'LL DAMAGE...

TODAY, I DID NOTHING BUT FALL DOWN...

...TRAINING TO BREAK MY FALL AND GET UP QUICKLY.

URO-KODAKI STANDS AGAINST ME...

...UN-ARMED.

I WIELD MY SWORD AND FACE UROKODAKI WITH THE INTENT TO STRIKE HIM DOWN.

HE EASILY THROWS ME TO THE GROUND.

HUUUH?!

BUT HE'S RIDICULOUSLY STRONG.

I'VE BEEN WRITING...

TODAY, I LEARNED BREATHING AND SOME STANDARD FORMS.

NO! NO! NO! THIS? THIS? LIKE THIS? NO!

...FOR SIX MONTHS, NEZUKO, AND YOU STILL HAVEN'T WOKEN UP.

HE SAID I DIDN'T HAVE ENOUGH STRENGTH IN MY CORE, THEN HE GOT ANGRY AND HIT MY STOMACH.

AAGH!

BAM

BAM

YET IT'S CLEARLY STRANGE FOR YOU TO KEEP SLEEPING LIKE THIS.

UROKODAKI IMMEDIATELY CALLED A DOCTOR TO LOOK AT YOU...

...BUT HE FOUND NOTHING WRONG.

AND...

...THAT'S STILL HOW I FEEL EVERY NIGHT.

I THOUGHT I'D WAKE UP IN THE MORNING TO FIND YOU DEAD.

I WAS SCARED.

MANY TIMES I'VE THOUGHT THAT I WOULD DIE.

AND EVERY DAY I GO HIGHER ON THE MOUNTAIN FOR MY TRAINING, EACH PLACE MORE DANGEROUS AND WITH THINNER AIR.

I HAVE NOTHING MORE TO TEACH YOU.

...THAT WAS ALL HE SAID.

ABOUT A YEAR AFTER I ARRIVED AT MOUNT SAGIRI...

HZZ

HZZ

HFF

HUH?

...TAKE WHAT I HAVE TAUGHT YOU AND BRING IT TO THE NEXT LEVEL?

CAN YOU...

THE REST IS UP TO YOU.

A BOULDER ....?

CAN YOU SPLIT IT WITH A KATANA?

CAN THAT EVEN BE SPLIT?!

I DON'T THINK I CAN.

THE BLADE WOULD BREAK.

UROKO-DAKI!!

UROKO-DAKI!

WAIT! THIS...

...HASN'T TAUGHT ME ANYTHING.

SINCE THAT DAY...

...UROKO-DAKI...

HOLDING MY BREATH, FLEXIBILITY, AND THE MOST BASIC THINGS TOO.

STILL...

I'M GLAD I WROTE EVERYTHING DOWN IN MY JOURNAL.

...EVERY DAY I PRACTICE WHAT I LEARNED FROM UROKO-DAKI.

I'M BEGINNING TO WORRY.

BUT EVEN AFTER HALF A YEAR I STILL CAN'T SPLIT THE BOULDER.

I HAVE TO DO MORE.

MORE!

I HAVEN'T HAD ENOUGH TRAINING.

IT ISN'T ENOUGH.

I CAN'T SMELL HIM!

A FOX MASK...?

WHERE DID HE COME FROM?!

?!

FWSH

WHATEVER THE SUFFERING, BEAR IT IN SILENCE.

IF YOU'RE A MAN.

OR ARE YOU STILL A LITTLE BOY?

!!

CHAPTER 5: TANJIRO'S JOURNAL, PART 2

WHAT ARE YOU DOING?

WHERE'D YOU COME FROM?!

!!

HOW LONG DO YOU PLAN TO HAVE YOUR BUTT STUCK IN THE MUD?

TAKE A STANCE!

DOING?

I'M TRAIN- ING.

NOW... ATTACK!

STOMP

...YOU HAVE A WOODEN SWORD AND I HAVE A REAL ONE!

BUT...

HA HA HA HA!

HA HA!

HA HA HA!

YOU'VE GAINED NOTHING. YOU HAVEN'T MASTERED ANYTHING!

YOU SPLIT A BOULDER?!

YOU JUST MEMORIZED IT AS A FACT...

BUT YOUR BODY DOESN'T *UNDER-STAND* ANYTHING!

TOTAL CONCEN-TRATION BREATHING!

CER-TAINLY NOT...

...THE BREATHING TECHNIQUE TAUGHT BY UROKODAKI!

HE KNOWS UROKODAKI?! AND ABOUT THE BREATHING...

!!

THUD

HMM.

FWP

I LEAVE THE REST TO YOU.

ARE YOU ALL RIGHT?

DID YOU SEE WHAT HAPPENED?

SH WF

THAT'S HOW I WANT TO BE TOO!

BUT IS THAT EVEN POSSIBLE?

CAN I DO IT...?

THAT WAS AN INCREDIBLE BLOW!

IT WAS TRULY BEAUTIFUL!

NOT A BIT OF UNNECESSARY MOTION!

UH... WHO ARE YOU?

SHE'S CUTE...

I'LL WATCH OVER YOU.

I'M SURE YOU CAN.

...AND TELLS ME THE GUY'S NAME IS SABITO.

SHE SAYS HER NAME IS MAKOMO...

SHE CORRECTS MY UNNECESSARY MOVEMENTS AND BAD HABITS.

MAKOMO POINTS OUT THE DEFECTS IN MY STYLE.

I ASK, BUT SHE NEVER TELLS ME.

WHERE DID SHE COME FROM?

WHY IS SHE DOING THIS FOR ME?

SHE OFTEN SAYS THOSE WORDS.

WE REALLY LIKE URO-KODAKI.

THERE ARE OTHER CHILDREN TOO.

THEY'RE ALL AROUND, WATCHING YOU.

THEY AREN'T SIBLINGS. THEY WERE BOTH ORPHANS.

UROKO-DAKI TOOK THEM IN AND RAISED THEM.

TOTAL CONCEN-TRATION BREATH-ING...

...ACCELERATES YOUR BLOOD FLOW AND HEARTBEAT.

AND YOUR TEMPERATURE SHOOTS UP.

MAKOMO IS A BIT OF A STRANGE GIRL.

SHE SAYS THINGS IN A WEIRD WAY.

...AND BRING...

...LOTS OF AIR INTO YOUR BLOOD.

YOU EXPAND YOUR LUNGS...

YOU'RE STILL HUMAN, BUT YOU GET STRONG LIKE A DEMON.

YOU GET HOT AND STRONG!

YOUR BLOOD GETS EXCITED AND YOUR BONES AND MUSCLES THRILL.

HOW CAN THAT BE?

I DON'T REALLY GET IT...

BASICALLY, I DON'T THINK THERE'S ANYTHING ELSE YOU CAN DO.

YOU MUST TRAIN SO HARD THAT YOU COULD DIE.

...BUT...

...AND HEART WOULD BURST IN MY CHEST...

...MY LUNGS...

...AND THAT...

...IT FELT LIKE MY ARMS AND LEGS WOULD COME OFF...

I SWUNG MY SWORD...

...SO HARD THAT...

...I STILL COULDN'T BEAT SABITO.

...HE HELD A REAL SWORD.

...WHEN I WENT TO FACE SABITO...

ANOTHER SIX MONTHS PASSED. UNTIL ONE DAY...

...AND I FOUND THAT MY SWORD HAD NOT CUT SABITO'S MASK.

IT HAD SPLIT THE BOULDER.

WORDS OF GRATITUDE

Thank you to everyone who read this work and to everyone who bought it. Thanks to your support, the series will continue. I can't tell you how thankful I am. Unlike water and food, manga isn't absolutely necessary for survival. Getting you to buy it is a tough job. Thank you very much. I create this manga with the help of many people. I'll work even harder to keep it interesting for you, so please keep reading. And again... thank you!!

Sorry...

I've gotten all your letters. Thank you. They make me so happy, but I can't reply, and that makes me very sorry. Forgive me, please. I'll keep doing my best!

HOWEVER, WHEN USING A NORMAL BLADE, EVEN CUTTING ITS NECK WON'T KILL IT.

A DEMON'S WEAK POINT IS ITS NECK.

THE SWORDS THAT THE DEMON SLAYER CORPS USE ARE MADE FROM A SPECIAL STEEL.

WE CALL THEM NICHIRIN SWORDS.

CHAPTER 6: A MOUNTAIN OF HANDS

WHEN I'M FIGHTING SOME-ONE...

...AND I FIND THAT SCENT, I SEE THE THREAD.

THANKS TO MY TRAINING WITH MAKOMO...

...I'VE LEARNED TO SMELL OUT AN "OPENING THREAD." THAT'S HOW I WON.

GUIDED BY THE THREAD, MY BLADE CUTS INTO THAT SPOT.

IT RUNS FROM MY BLADE...

...TO A SPOT ON MY OPPONENT, AND IT GOES TAUT THE MOMENT I SEE IT.

I HAD NO WISH TO SEE ANOTHER CHILD DIE.

I DIDN'T THINK YOU WOULD SPLIT THAT BOULDER...

I DID NOT INTEND TO SEND YOU TO FINAL SELECTION.

...BUT YOU DID WELL.

...ARE AN AMAZING CHILD.

TANJIRO ...

...YOU...

...BUT BE SURE TO RETURN ALIVE.

GO TO FINAL SELECTION...

YOUR SISTER AND I ARE HERE WAITING.

IT'S CALLED A WARDING MASK.

AFTER CUTTING MY HAIR...

APPARENTLY, IT OFFERS PROTECTION FROM EVIL.

UROKODAKI GAVE ME A MASK.

SO I'M LEAVING HER IN UROKODAKI'S CARE.

I CAN'T TAKE NEZUKO WITH ME—SHE'S STILL ASLEEP.

I'M ON MY WAY, UROKODAKI!

GIVE MY BEST TO SABITO AND MAKOMO!

TANJIRO...

...HOW IS IT YOU...

...KNOW THE NAMES OF THOSE DECEASED CHILDREN?

MOUNT FUJIKASANE: SITE OF FINAL SELECTION

WOW!

BUT WISTERIA...

...SHOULDN'T BE BLOOMING THIS TIME OF YEAR.

LOOK HOW MANY THERE ARE!

THE ONE WHO KILLS HIM FIRST GETS TO EAT HIM!

IT'S BEEN SO LONG SINCE I TASTED HUMAN FLESH!

WATER BREATHING!

TOTAL CONCEN-TRATION ...

I'VE GOTTEN STRONGER.

I BEAT TWO DEMONS!

DID IT.

...I CAN DO THIS!

ALL THAT TRAINING WORKED...

REST IN PEACE!

...EVEN THE BONES CRUMBLE!

WHEN I USE THE KATANA THAT URO-KODAKI GAVE ME...

KR RK SH

WHAT'S THAT ROTTEN SMELL?

UGH!

SNIFF

I'VE NEVER SEEN ANYTHING LIKE IT!

THERE'S A HUGE, DEFORMED DEMON BACK THERE!

THMP

WAAAH!

WVSH

I'M NOT POWERLESS ANYMORE!

LET'S GO!

HELP HIM! I MUST HELP HIM!

DON'T BE AFRAID!

WATER BREATH-ING

SECOND FORM:

WATER WHEEL!

...FOXES HAS COME!

ANOTHER OF MY DEAR...

GLARE

CHAPTER 7: SPIRITS OF THE DECEASED

DO YOU THINK...

...TANJIRO CAN REALLY DO IT?

SABITO ...?

AND YOU KNOW THAT...

...RIGHT?

...NO AMOUNT OF EFFORT IS TOO MUCH.

BUT...

I DON'T KNOW.

WOOOE

DAMN UROKO-DAKI!

DAMN UROKO-DAKI!

DAMN UROKO-DAKI!

DAMN HIM!

BRBL

BLRB

...

GAAAGH!

AGAIN AND AGAIN!

ALL WHILE I'VE BEEN TRAPPED HERE!

UNFORGIVABLE! UNFORGIVABLE!

IT'S BEEN 47 TORTUROUS YEARS!

OH, I KNOW HIM! UROKODAKI WAS THE ONE WHO CAPTURED ME! I WILL NEVER FORGET!

YOU KNOW URO—

IN THE EDO PERIOD... THE KEIO ERA!

BACK THEN HE WAS STILL A DEMON SLAYER!

NO DEMON HERE HAS BEEN ALIVE THAT LONG!

LIES!

YOU'RE LYING!

DEMON HUNTER... EDO PERIOD?!

PLUS, THE DEMONS EAT EACH OTHER TOO!

...AND THEY GET KILLED DURING SELECTION!

THEY ONLY PUT DEMONS UP HERE THAT HAVE EATEN TWO OR THREE PEOPLE...

...I HAVE EATEN 50 OF YOU BRATS!

...OF WISTERIA BLOSSOMS...

BUT I HAVE SURVIVED A VERY LONG TIME. IN THIS PRISON...

...A DEMON'S STRENGTH COMES FROM THE NUMBER OF PEOPLE IT HAS CONSUMED.

REMEMBER...

FIFTY?!

...AND SOME PHYSICALLY CHANGE, GAINING UNNATURAL POWERS.

THAT'S RIGHT. THEY GROW STRONGER...

IF IT EATS MANY PEOPLE IT GETS STRONGER?

...HOW MANY PEOPLE A DEMON HAS EATEN.

IF YOUR NOSE GETS STRONGER YOU'LL BE ABLE TO TELL...

?!

WHAT ARE YOU TALKING ABOUT?

...YOU ARE NUMBER 14.

...12...

...13...

...AND...

I'VE DECIDED TO KILL *ALL* OF HIS STUDENTS!

THAT'S HOW MANY OF *UROKODAKI'S STUDENTS* I HAVE EATEN!

HEE HEE

HEE HEE

HEE

THE OTHER WAS A GIRL-BRAT WHOSE KIMONO WAS COVERED IN FLOWERS.

SHE WAS SMALL AND NOT SO STRONG...

...BUT SHE WAS VERY AGILE.

HE HAD A COLORFUL JACKET, AND WAS THE STRONGEST BY FAR.

HE HAD PEACH-COLORED HAIR AND A SCAR BY HIS MOUTH.

THIRTEEN OF URO-KADAKI'S STUDENTS, BUT ABOVE ALL...

YES, INDEED!

...TWO OF THEM...

...I'LL NEVER FORGET.

HOW COULD THIS DEMON HAVE KILLED THEM? THEY TRAINED ME!

I KNOW THE GRAIN OF THOSE MASKS THAT UROKO-DAKI CARVES.

THEY'RE CARVED THE SAME WAY AS THE TENGU MASK HE WORE.

I RECOGNIZE YOU...

...BY THOSE FOX MASKS.

THEY'RE ALL INSIDE MY STOMACH.

IT'S LIKE UROKODAKI FED THEM TO ME!

DID HE CALL IT A "WARDING MASK"?

I ATE THEM ALL *BECAUSE* OF THE MASKS THEY WORE.

THE GIRL-BRAT WEPT AND GREW ANGRY WHEN I TOLD HER THAT.

HEH HEH HEH HEH...

HEH HEH...

HEH HEH HEH HEH...

THE FOX-
BRAT
IS IN
STRIKING
RANGE!

I CAN'T
GROW
MORE IN
TIME!

AND I'M
OUT OF
HANDS!

HE
ESCAPED!

WATER
BREATHING!

TOTAL
CONCENTRA-
TION.

EVEN THE
PEACH-
HAIR
COULDN'T
CUT IT!

BUT MY
NECK IS
HARD AND
IMPERVI-
OUS!

...AND
CRUSH IT,
JUST LIKE
I DID TO
THE OTHER
ONE!

WHEN HE
FAILS TO
CUT MY
NECK, I'LL
GRAB HIS
HEAD...

SNIFF

THE BOULDER THAT TANJIRO CUT WAS BIGGER AND HARDER THAN ANYONE HAD EVER CUT BEFORE!

HRAAAAH!!

YOU'RE READING THE
WRONG WAY!

DEMON SLAYER: KIMETSU NO YAIBA reads from right to left, starting in the upper-right corner. Japanese is read from right to left, meaning that action, sound effects and word-balloon order are completely reversed from English order.